Walt Whitman: The Life and Legacy of One of America's Most Influential Poets

By Charles River Editors

About Charles River Editors

Charles River Editors is a boutique digital publishing company, specializing in bringing history back to life with educational and engaging books on a wide range of topics. Keep up to date with our new and free offerings with this 5 second sign up on our weekly mailing list, and visit Our Kindle Author Page to see other recently published Kindle titles.

We make these books for you and always want to know our readers' opinions, so we encourage you to leave reviews and look forward to publishing new and exciting titles each week.

Introduction

Walt Whitman

"The proof of a poet is that his country absorbs him as affectionately as he has absorbed it." – Walt Whitman

Walt Whitman, the great American poet, is also in many ways a great American enigma, for more and less are known about him than other famous men in 19th century American history. On the one hand, he was the product of something of an all-American family, the sort of salt of the earth people he would later describe so vividly in his work. On the other, he was a complete bohemian and profligate, given to vanity in the way he dressed and lived. He started out his career as a school teacher and was later a newspaper man, but he left both those types of work for a job as a government bureaucrat. As a young man, when most of his peers were sowing their wild oats, he was considered by many to be a stick in the mud who neither drank nor chased women. Then, as a middle-aged man, when his peers had settled down into quieter lives, he remained single and seems to have pursued romantic relationships with both men and women.

Then, of course, there was his poetry, words that summarized both the best and worst about his nation. His seminal work, *Leaves of Grass*, began as little more than a pamphlet but grew for decades, as each new edition added more poems. By the time of his death, it had become a large volume still studied today. While he wrote other pieces for publication, *Leaves of Grass* remained his magnum opus and his baby, nurturing and developing it throughout his life. And yet, through it all, the title remained the same self-deprecating play on words that he had given it when he first self-published the work in 1855.

Floyd Stovall, who published a collection of Whitman's works in 1933, explained how Whitman's life and work affected the society around him: "Whitman, like the age that produced him, was both a culmination and a beginning. In him was the flower of romantic idealism in America, which had its roots in the eighteenth-century philosophy of progress, and in him also the seed of scientific realism, which throws its maze of branches about contemporary thought. He bridges the chasm made by the Civil War between the idealism of the past and the materialism of the present and thus becomes the representative of united America…Yet he was never popular. In the passionate conflicts of a changing civilization, the advocate of harmony is liable to be suspected by all factions. So it was with Whitman. The realist distrusted his faith in humanity, and the idealist was shocked because he extolled the animalism of man. On the one hand, he allowed his readers no escape from the imperfections of the world, while on the other he required them to transcend these imperfections. The popular writer, however, must be one who enables his readers to retain their faith in the actual world by obscuring its imperfections in the twilight of sentiment and fancy."

Walt Whitman: The Life and Legacy of One of America's Most Influential Poets looks at the life and times of 19th century America's most controversial poet and the impact his famous work had. Along with pictures depicting important people, places, and events, you will learn about Walt Whitman like never before.

Walt Whitman: The Life and Legacy of One of America's Most Influential Poets

About Charles River Editors

Introduction

  A Start in Publishing

  Wading into Politics

  The American Poet

  The Civil War Years

  Later Years

  Online Resources

  Bibliography

Free Books by Charles River Editors

Discounted Books by Charles River Editors

A Start in Publishing

"To me, every hour of the day and night is an unspeakably perfect miracle." – Walt Whitman

Walter Whitman was born in the West Hills neighborhood of Huntington, Long Island on May 31, 1819. His parents, Walter and Louisa, were Quakers but not very devout in their practice. According to author Floyd Stovall, Walter (who was called Walt at home to distinguish him from his father) "was of mixed English, Dutch, and Welsh stock, and…his family, long resident on Long Island, had been for two generations much under the influence of the Quaker preacher, Elias Hicks…An important but incalculable influence may be found in the diffused thought and speculation of the age, which he would inevitably come to know in the course of his intellectual development. … The aspects of this movement that are most clearly reflected in the thought of Walt Whitman were (1) the philosophy of progress, with its a priori method of reform and neglect of history; (2) faith in the innate goodness of man and the idealization of nature, illustrated in the revolutionary theories of Rousseau; (3) the idealism of German philosophy, particularly the Hegelian doctrine of a cosmic consciousness that unfolds through conflict and contradiction to divine ends; and (4) the scientific conception of nature as a reality independent of cosmic reason but determined by the processes of historical evolution."

Young Walt joined one year old Jesse and was in turn, in the years that followed, joined by seven other brothers and sisters. When Walt was four years old, the growing family moved to Brooklyn, the first of many moves that would be brought on by his father's reckless ways with money. Walt later recalled, "From 1824 to '28 our family lived in Brooklyn in Front, Cranberry and Johnson streets. In the latter my father built a nice house for a home, and afterwards another in Tillary street. We occupied them, one after the other, but they were mortgaged, and we lost them."

Money issues aside, things at home were good for young Walt. Indeed, he always recalled with joy the time he was lifted by the aging war hero, the Marquis de Lafayette, and given a kiss by the Frenchman. John Burroughs later described the scene: "On the visit of General Lafayette to this country, in 1824, he came over to Brooklyn in state, and rode through the city. The children of the schools turn'd out to join in the welcome. An edifice for a free public library for youths was just then commencing, and Lafayette consented to stop on his way and lay the corner-stone. Numerous children arriving on the ground, where a huge irregular excavation for the building was already dug, surrounded with heaps of rough stone, several gentlemen assisted in lifting the children to safe or convenient spots to see the ceremony. Among the rest, Lafayette, also helping the children, took up the five-year-old Walt Whitman, and pressing the child a moment to his breast, and giving him a kiss, handed him down to a safe spot in the excavation."

Lafayette

Whitman received most of his education from public schools in the area, but he concluded his formal education in 1830, when he went to work as an office boy for a local team of attorneys. He remembered his time there fondly, writing, "I had a nice desk and window-nook to myself; Edward C[larke]. kindly help'd me at my handwriting and composition, and, (the signal event of my life up to that time,) subscribed for me to a big circulating library. For a time I now revel'd in romance-reading of all kinds; first, the 'Arabian Nights,' all the volumes, an amazing treat. Then, with sorties in very many other directions, took in Walter Scott's novels, one after another, and his poetry, (and continue to enjoy novels and poetry to this day.)"

Sir Walter Scott

Later, Whitman left the law office to apprentice with the *Long Island Patriot*, and he mastered much of the publishing trade before moving on to work at the print shop of Erastus Worthington in Brooklyn. He then worked at the *Long-Island Star*. It was during this that Whitman began to enjoy the life of a young man living in 19th century New York City, which included joining the local debating society and lending library. He even had some of his work published in the *New York Mirror*.

Though he had quite a resume by the time he was 16 years old, Whitman fell on hard times when a massive fire swept through the New York paper district, wiping out printers and newspapers alike. Thus, in May 1836, he was forced to move back in with his parents, who by this time were living in Hempstead, Long Island. He found work there as a teacher, a job he did not enjoy, and he gave it up as soon as he had saved enough money to return to Huntington. Investing every dime he had managed to save, he founded his own newspaper, which he named the *Long-Islander*. He was barely 20 years old when, 10 months later, he sold the paper to E.O. Crowell and went to work at the *Long Island Democrat* under Editor James J. Brenton. According to Professor Emory Holloway, the 20th century author of "Uncollected Poetry and Prose of Walt Whitman," "Mrs. Brenton always emphasized, when speaking of Whitman, that he was inordinately indolent and lazy and had a very pronounced disinclination to work! During some of the time he was in the household the apple trees in the garden were in bloom. When Whitman would come from the printing office and finish the mid-day dinner he would go out into the garden, lie on his back under the apple tree and forget everything about going back to work as he gazed up at the blossoms and the sky. Frequently at such times Mr. Brenton would wait for him at the office for an hour or two and then send the 'printer's devil' up to the house to see what had become of him. He would invariably be found still lying on his back on the grass looking into the tree, entirely oblivious of the fact that he was expected to be at work. When spoken to he would get up reluctantly and go slowly back to the shop. At the end of such a day Mr. Brenton would come home and say, Walt has been of very little help to me today. I wonder what I can do to make him realize that he must work for a living?' and Mrs. Brenton would remark, 'I don't see why he doesn't catch his death of cold lying there on the ground under that apple tree!' And, lying there under the apple trees, in seeming indolence what great thoughts were being slowly matured in that prolific brain?"

Given that characterization of the young man, it is easy enough to understand why Whitman returned to teaching from 1840-41.

Wading into Politics

Whitman around the age of 28

"Have you learned the lessons only of those who admired you, and were tender with you, and stood aside for you? Have you not learned great lessons from those who braced themselves against you, and disputed passage with you?" – Walt Whitman

Though he would later scandalize many, Whitman was considered an upstanding young man in his early years. For instance, he often spoke out in favor of temperance, boring his friends with screeds against liquor. He had tried alcohol briefly in his youth and did not find it to his liking, so he he threw his considerable talents into the nation's earliest prohibition movement. In 1842 he published a "temperance novel" called *Franklin Evans*, and in it he warned, "Young men, in our cities, think much more of dress than they do of decent behavior. You will find, when you go among them, that whatever remains of integrity you have, will be laughed and ridiculed out of you. It is considered 'green' not to be up to all kinds of dissipation, and familiar with debauchery and intemperance. And it is the latter which will assail you on every side, and which, if you yield to it, will send you back from the city, a bloated and weak creature, to die among your country friends, and be laid in a premature grave; or which will too soon end your days in some miserable street in the city itself. It is indeed a dangerous step!"

In the years that followed the publication of *Franklin Evans*, Whitman's tastes changed, and so did his views on liquor in turn. Much later in life, he even claimed to despise his earlier work on behalf of the temperance movement, telling someone in 1888, "I doubt if there is a copy in existence: I have none and have not had one for years; it was a pamphlet. Parke Godwin and another somebody (who was it?) came to see me about writing it. Their offer of cash payment was so tempting—I was so hard up at the time—that I set to work at once ardently on it (with the help of a bottle of port or what not). In three days of constant work I finished the book. Finished the book? Finished myself. It was damned rot—rot of the worst sort—not insincere, perhaps, but rot, nevertheless: it was not the business for me to be up to. I stopped right there: I never cut a chip off that kind of timber again."

While Whitman may have preferred to remember himself as having never being an advocate of temperance, plenty of evidence suggests otherwise, including several other pieces he wrote during this time in which he advocated abstinence from all forms of alcohol.

Although he seems to have abandoned some of his early beliefs about alcohol, there were plenty of other views to which Whitman held steadfast. The most significant of these was his early and ongoing opposition to slavery. Despite the attempt to settle America's slavery issue with the Missouri Compromise in 1820, the young nation kept pushing further westward, and with that, more territory was acquired. After the Mexican-American War ended in 1848, the sectional crisis was brewing like never before, with California and the newly-acquired Mexican territory now ready to be organized into states. The country was once again left trying to figure out how to do it without offsetting the slave-free state balance that was already dividing the nation. With the new territory acquired in the Mexican-American War, pro and anti-slavery groups were at an impasse. The Whig Party, including a freshman Congressman named Abraham Lincoln, supported the Wilmot Proviso, which would have banned slavery in all territory acquired from Mexico, but the slave states would have none of it. Even after Texas was annexed as a slave state, the enormous new territory would doubtless contain many other new states, and the North hoped to limit slavery as much as possible in the new territories.

Whitman supported the Wilmot Proviso, but at the same time, he did not consider himself an abolitionist, complaining that "there appears a kind of vindictiveness, a want of charity, a disposition to ultraism which must be highly offensive to persons of correct views." Over time, Whitman wanted to see slavery done away with altogether, but his evolution on the stance of abolition took time and heightened maturity, two things he benefitted from when he returned to working for newspapers. According to biographer David Reynolds, Whitman "began writing for literary magazines; he edited at least one paper, the Aurora, for a month in 1842; and he freelanced for a number of others, including the Evening Tattler, the New York Sun, the New York Mirror, and the Brooklyn Evening Star. For almost two years, from 1846 to 1848, he was the editor of the Eagle. The issues he championed there in editorials, as well as in poems and short fiction, included opposition to the death penalty, improved schools, fairer wages for sewing women, personal hygiene, and temperance."

In trying to determine Whitman's earliest political leanings, Reynolds noted, "Generally, what has been unearthed suggests a political moderate who asked for a fair chance for his own class but nothing more. Perhaps he believed that their 'average' status was what made the working classes politically 'divine,' their lack of political and social power involuntarily distancing them from the materialism that blinded their capitalist 'landlords.' ... In what was later entitled 'To Think of Time,' he describes a stage driver who died-- not particularly 'young' for the time--at age forty--one. Neither socially oppressed nor absolutely impoverished, he succumbed mainly to his voracious love of life."

Still, Whitman's politics would ultimately cost him his job, for he made the mistake in 1848 of opposing his bosses at the *Eagle* and siding with "Barnburners," a group of New York Democrats who split their party's platform by opposing slavery. Whitman lost his job at the paper in 1848, the same year he served as a delegate to the Barnburner's new Free Soil Party. The split also cost the Democrats the White House and put Zachary Taylor in office.

The American Poet

"I believe a leaf of grass is no less than the journey-work of the stars." – Walt Whitman

On the surface, it may have looked like politics caused career problems, but by this time Whitman was already having his work regularly published in various periodicals in the area. Among these was a draft of a newspaper article he entitled "Nerve," which included the following: "A Frenchman named...a voyager in a balloon from the Military Garden in Brooklyn, rested simply on a narrow triangle with cross pieces of sticks.—On these, away up in the air and even when we could only see him well by the aid of glasses, he would swing down like a monkey in that vast emptiness, holding on merely by his hands, and drawing himself up again, and turning somersets as nimbly as a cat."

In 1852, Whitman got his first big break when he was hired to serialize *The Life and Adventures of Jack Engle: An Auto-Biography: A Story of New York at the Present Time in which the Reader Will Find Some Familiar Characters* for *The Sunday Dispatch*. In 2017 Zachary Turpin observed of this work, "The story of Jack Engle will seem both vaguely familiar and exceedingly strange to readers, I imagine. Formally, it is a short novel (or long tale) of about 36,000 words, a story of coincidence, adventure, and the incompatibility of love and greed. Though formulaic at times (like many of Whitman's earlier fictions), Jack Engle is also beautifully lyrical, occasionally hilarious, and peopled throughout with charmingly eccentric characters. It is some of the better fiction Whitman produced."

A RICH REVELATION.—This week's SUNDAY DISPATCH will contain the LIFE AND ADVENTURES OF JACK ENGLE, an Auto-Biography, in which will be handled the Philosophy, Philanthropy, Pauperism, Law, Crime, Love, Matrimony. Morals, &c., which are characteristic of this great City at the present time, including the Manners and Morals of Boarding Houses. some Scenes from Church History, Operations in Wall-st., with graphic Sketches of Men and Women. as they appear to the public, and as they appear in other scenes not public. Read it and you will find some familiar cases and characters, with explanations necessary to properly understand what it is all about.   m13-1t

A newspaper advertisement of the work

The novella, which was published in six installments, aptly represented Whitman's style. As Turpin noted, "Whitman himself is probably best categorized as a sentimentalist. The influence of this tradition on his writings has only recently garnered much attention, probably due…to the general critical under emphasis of Whitman's fiction. Regardless, his stories nearly always foreground 'sentimental topoi,' which…include 'death, broken families, childhood innocence, and transcendent love'-to which I would add themes like bodily suffering, empathy, and social reform…In Whitman's fiction, such themes yield character resolutions that are almost invariably neat: the guilty are punished, the greedy impoverished, the innocent or repentant redeemed, and the parted reunited by coincidence. Jack Engle rarely veers from these well-polished tracks, though when it does the detours can be quite surprising."

To illustrate this point, Turpin explained, "As the story's plucky orphan and protagonist-narrator, Jack recounts his early life as one of hardship.... The reader is given to understand that Jack would be shuffling even now, had his life not been relieved by the generosity of others. Those kindest to him are the poor (shopkeepers, clerks, office boys, and fellow orphans) or marginalized (dancers, madames, gambling house owners). ...Jack's adoption is a key episode, one that will propel him into the complicated adult world of employment, crime, and romance. His entry into the study of law provides the necessary conflict: true to Whitman's plot notes, Jack's employer, the aptly named Mr. Covert, is gradually revealed to be an unrepentant villain, scheming after the inheritance of his ward-that is, his adopted daughter-Martha. With the help of a merry band of friends, Jack sets out to save Martha, whose past he finds intriguingly bound up with his own."

Though he likely appreciated the money he earned from these efforts, Whitman had already moved on to a bigger project, one that would shape the course of the rest of his life. It was a small collection of poetry he would call *Leaves of Grass*, and he began work on it almost on a dare. The impetus behind the work came from an 1844 essay by Ralph Waldo Emerson, in which the famous Transcendentalist complained about contemporary society but also challenged it: "We have yet had no genius in America, with tyrannous eye, which knew the value of our incomparable materials, and saw, in the barbarism and materialism of the times, another carnival of the same gods whose picture he so much admires in Homer; then in the middle age; then in Calvinism. Banks and tariffs, the newspaper and caucus, Methodism and Unitarianism, are flat and dull to dull people, but rest on the same foundations of wonder as the town of Troy, and the temple of Delphos, and are as swiftly passing away. Our logrolling, our stumps and their politics, our fisheries, our Negroes, and Indians, our boasts, and our repudiations, the wrath of rogues, and the pusillanimity of honest men, the northern trade, the southern planting, the western clearing, Oregon, and Texas, are yet unsung. Yet America is a poem in our eyes; its ample geography dazzles the imagination, and it will not wait long for metres. If I have not found that excellent combination of gifts in my countrymen which I seek, neither could I aid myself to fix the idea of the poet by reading now and then in Chalmers's collection of five centuries of English poets. These are wits, more than poets, though there have been poets among them."

Emerson

The first edition of *Leaves of Grass* contained only 12 poems, written on 95 small pages. The introduction made up nearly a fifth of the book, and it contained Whitman's musings on his work. None of the poems had titles, so they are typically distinguished and referenced by their first lines. The longest poem, later called "Song of Myself," made up over half of the actual text, with the other 11 poems being of more typical length.

An engraving of Whitman on the frontispiece to *Leaves of Grass*

There was a reason the collection was so small. Whitman himself later explained, "I have long teased my brain with visions of a handsome little book at last…for the pocket. That would tend to induce people to take me along with them and read me in the open air: I am nearly always successful with the reader in the open air. I have my own peculiar affection for November Boughs. It is the depository of many dreams and thoughts precious to me — of many sacred aspirational experiences, too holy to be argued about — of sayings, almost of mots: of so many unspeakable records, reminiscences, worked into the soil of my matured life and now at last projected in this compact shape. To have such a book — such a book produced in every way according to a feller's simple and unimpeded humors — that has been my idea, is still my idea."

By this time, Whitman was well-known in literary circles, and his work, *November Boughs*, merited a review and interview in *The New York Herald*. In that paper, reporter David McKay wrote, "This book is as varied in contents as its author's own mind. In it the reader will find poems, essays, biographies (these being of preachers only), war memoranda and extracts from diaries. Many of the poems have already been seen by the Herald's readers, being first published in these columns. ... Everything in this book is interesting, though the portion which will probably be most closely read is the author's sketch of himself and his literary purposes. Necessarily it impels large mention of 'Leaves of Grass,' the best abused volume of verse ever published, 'Don Juan' not excepted."

In *November Boughs*, Whitman did indeed fall back on his most famous work, musing, "Behind all else that can be said, I consider 'Leaves of Grass' and its theory experimental—as, in the deepest sense, I consider our American Republic itself to be, with its theory. ... In the second place, the volume is a sortie—whether to prove triumphant, and conquer its field of aim and escape and construction, nothing less than a hundred years from now can fully answer. I consider the point that I have positively gained a hearing to far more than make up for any and all other lacks and withholdings. Essentially, that was from the first, and has remained throughout, the main object. Now it seems to be achieved, I am certainly contented to waive any otherwise momentous drawbacks as of little account...Candidly and dispassionately reviewing all my intentions, I feel that they were creditable—and I accept the result, whatever it may be."

While the title *Leaves of Grass* sounds elegant and maybe even mysterious to the modern reader, Whitman had no such intentions when he chose it. Instead, it was a play on words based on his experiences in the newspaper and printing worlds. "Leaves" was a common term for pages of a book, while "Grass" was a derogatory term used by publishers to describe pieces that were not very highly valued or respected. Ironically, Whitman's family agreed with his evaluation of the work; his brother George later wrote, "I was about twenty-five then. I saw the book—didn't read it all—didn't think it worth reading—fingered it a little. Mother thought as I did—did not know what to make of it."

Whitman registered his future masterpiece with the United States District Court in New Jersey on May 15, 1855, securing a copyright prior to its publication and release on July 4. Instead of listing himself on the cover or even the flyleaf as the author, he had an engraving of himself placed at the beginning of the book, and later, in one of the poems, he revealed his name. In "I Celebrate Myself," he wrote, "Walt Whitman, an American, one of the roughs, a kosmos, Disorderly, fleshy, sensual, eating, drinking, breeding, No sentimentalist, no stander above men and women, or apart from them—no more modest than immodest." Depending on one's perspective, this could have been either an act of supreme humility or arrogance.

Though he sent a copy of his book to Emerson as soon as it was published, Whitman later denied that Emerson was the only catalyst to his work, insisting, "I was simmering, simmering, simmering; Emerson brought me to a boil." Emerson replied to Whitman's gift by writing, "I am not blind to the worth of the wonderful gift of 'LEAVES OF GRASS.' I find it the most extraordinary piece of wit and wisdom that America has yet contributed. I am very happy in reading it, as great power makes us happy. It meets the demand I am always making of what seemed the sterile and stingy nature, as if too much handiwork, or too much lymph in the temperament, were making our western wits fat and mean. I give you joy of your free and brave thought. I have great joy in it. I find incomparable things said incomparably well, as they must be. I find the courage of treatment which so delights us, and which large perception only can inspire." Emerson concluded, "I greet you at the beginning of a great career, which yet must have had a long foreground somewhere, for such a start. I rubbed my eyes a little, to see if this sunbeam were no illusion; but the solid sense of the book is a sober certainty. It has the best merits, namely, of fortifying and encouraging."

Whitman, financing the book's printing himself, could only afford a first run of 800 copies. In his introduction, he observed, "AMERICA does not repel the past or what it has produced under its forms or amid other politics or the idea of castes or the old religions...accepts the lesson with calmness...is not so impatient as has been supposed that the slough still sticks to opinions and manners and literature while the life which served its requirements has passed into the new life of the new forms...perceives that the corpse is slowly borne from the eating and sleeping rooms of the house...perceives that it waits a little while in the door...that it was fittest for its days...that its action has descended to the stalwart and well-shaped heir who approaches...and that he shall be fittest for his days."

Words like these eventually moved many readers to label Whitman "America's poet," but the poems he published made a stir from the very beginning. Whitman was moved by Emerson's work and that of other Transcendentalist authors to express himself in ways that were considered scandalous in antebellum America. For example, consider his words in the second section of "I Sing the Body Electric:"

"The love of the body of man or woman balks account, the body itself balks account,

That of the male is perfect, and that of the female is perfect.

The expression of the face balks account,

But the expression of a well-made man appears not only in his face,

It is in his limbs and joints also, it is curiously in the joints of his hips and wrists,

It is in his walk, the carriage of his neck, the flex of his waist and knees, dress does not hide him,

The strong sweet quality he has strikes through the cotton and broadcloth,

To see him pass conveys as much as the best poem, perhaps more,

You linger to see his back, and the back of his neck and shoulder-side."

If his description of the male body upset many of his contemporaries, his description of the female form left them apoplectic: "The sprawl and fulness of babes, the bosoms and heads of women, the folds of their dress, their style as we pass in the street, the contour of their shape downwards/The swimmer naked in the swimming-bath, seen as he swims through the transparent green-shine, or lies with his face up and rolls silently to and fro in the heave of the water,"

Worst of all, of course, were the words that seemed to be thinly veiled references to homosexuality:

> "The wrestle of wrestlers, two apprentice-boys, quite grown, lusty, good-natured, native-born, out on the vacant lot at sun-down after work,
>
> The coats and caps thrown down, the embrace of love and resistance,
>
> The upper-hold and under-hold, the hair rumpled over and blinding the eyes;
>
> The march of firemen in their own costumes, the play of masculine muscle through clean-setting trowsers and waist-straps,
>
> The slow return from the fire, the pause when the bell strikes suddenly again, and the listening on the alert,
>
> The natural, perfect, varied attitudes, the bent head, the curv'd neck and the counting;
>
> Such-like I love—I loosen myself, pass freely, am at the mother's breast with the little child,
>
> Swim with the swimmers, wrestle with wrestlers, march in line with the firemen, and pause, listen, count."

Those who did not find Whitman's sexual references offensive found his personal references irritating. One of his first critics complained, "The reader who has proceeded only thus far begins already to discover that Walter Whitman is a pantheist. ... With-out knowing how to chop the formal logic of the schools, he is a necessitarian and fatalist, with whom "whatever is is right." The world as he finds it, and man as he is, good or bad, high or low, ignorant or learned, holy or vicious, are all alike good enough for Walter Whitman, who is in himself a "kosmos," and whose emotional nature is at once the sensorium of humanity and the sounding board which catches up and intones each note of joy or sorrow in the "gamut of human feeling."

The critic next honed in on Whitman's now famous portrayal of himself as an "every man," writing, ""He represents himself as being alike of the old and the young, of the foolish as much as the wise; maternal in his instincts as well as paternal; a child as well as a man; a Southerner as soon as a Northerner; a planter, nonchalant and hospitable; a Yankee, bound his own way and ever ready for a swap; a Kentuckian, walking the trail of the Elkhorn with deerskin leggings; a boatman over the lakes or bays or along coasts; a Hoosier, a Badger, a Wolverine, a Buckeye, a Louisianian, a 'poke-easy' from sandhills and pines: at home equally on the hills of Vermont, or in the woods of Maine, or the Texas ranch; a learner with the simplest, a teacher of the thoughtfulest, a farmer, mechanic, or artist, a gentleman, sailor, lover, or quaker, a prisoner, fancy-man, rowdy, lawyer, physician, or priest."

While many whispered questions or made ribald jokes, only a few dared speak their concerns aloud. Among the most prominent of the critics was Rufus W. Griswold, himself a popular poet. In reviewing *Leaves of Grass*, he wrote, "In our allusion to this book, we have found it impossible to convey any, even the most faithful idea of its style and contents, and of our disgust and detestation of them, without employing language that cannot be pleasing to ears polite; but it does seem that some one should, under circumstances like these, undertake a most disagreeable, yet stern duty. The records of crime show that many monsters have gone on in impunity, because the exposure of their vileness was attended with too great indelicacy. Peccatum illud hobbibile, inter Christianos non nominandum." The Latin phrase translates in English to "That horrible sin not to be mentioned among Christians." It was a reference, of course, to homosexuality.

Griswold

By the time the reviews began to pour in, the work's publisher had already gone out on a limb and printed a second edition of the book. Whitman added 20 additional poems to this edition, making it a more standard sized tome. However, when the publisher read what was being said about *Leaves of Grass*, he delayed releasing it and considered accepting his losses instead of further angering the reading public. Finally, with the encouragement of Whitman and others, the second edition was released to the retail market in August 1856.

In spite of the book's success, Whitman did not make enough from the first two editions to live off of, so he had to return to working for a newspaper, this time as editor of the *Brooklyn Daily Times*, in May 1857. In 1858 Whitman, using the pen name Mose Velsor, published a series entitled "Manly Health and Training," shocking many of his readers by advocating nudity for both sun bathing and daily cold baths, as well as an early version of the Paleo diet. He further recommended wearing beards and comfortable shoes.

Bathing in the nude was the most scandalous part of the work. Whitman wrote, "Never before did I get so close to Nature; never before did she come so close to me… Nature was naked, and I was also… Sweet, sane, still Nakedness in Nature! – ah if poor, sick, prurient humanity in cities might really know you once more! Is not nakedness indecent? No, not inherently. It is your thought, your sophistication, your fear, your respectability, that is indecent. There come moods when these clothes of ours are not only too irksome to wear, but are themselves indecent."

"Manly Health and Training" was not well-received and became a source of derision in the years that followed. It is not surprising, therefore, that this period in Whitman's life saw him transition from aspiring journalist to inspired poet, and he left the newspaper business once and for all in 1859. According to Reynolds, "The three influences most often credited for Whitman's transformation from journalist to poet are Emerson, the Italian opera, and the New Testament. From the first, he got his vision of the born- again individualist; through the second, this self-reliant vision was dramatized and heightened through the sound of the human voice on the operatic stage; and from the third, he absorbed the altruistic spirit of the Bible's central character, Jesus Christ. But we must add to this trinity…the turbulence of the times over the question of slavery, which led to the Civil War and Whitman's Christ-like mission in the military hospitals in Washington."

The Civil War Years

"The real war will never get in the books." – Walt Whitman

Whitman spent much of his time in the 1850s revising *Leaves of Grass*, which was released again in a new edition in 1860. This one was 456 pages long, far from the "small book" of 1850, and contained 146 new poems. He also revised some of his previous poems and divided the book into groups called clusters. Among the clusters of poems were "Chants Democratic and Native American," "Calamus," and "Enfans d'Adam." This volume was also much more elaborately printed. According to author Gregory Eiselein, it "appeared in a variety of differently-colored cloth bindings—orange, green, and brown—many embossed with decorative designs. The book's pages were well-printed in a clear ten-point type on heavy white paper and elaborately decorated with line-drawings around titles and the beginning and end of poems. The title page and the poem titles appear in various fonts and sizes, and some—like the script-like typography of the title page—are fancy. Scattered throughout the volume are small illustrations of a butterfly perched on a human finger, a sunrise, and a globe resting on a cloud and revealing the Western hemisphere. The frontispiece is an engraving by Stephen Alonzo Schoff from an oil painting portrait by Charles Hine; it depicts Whitman not as a working-class rough as in the 1855 frontispiece but as a well-coiffured and genteel romantic poet wearing a large, loose silk cravat. In its advertisements, Thayer and Eldridge highlighted the book's elegant design."

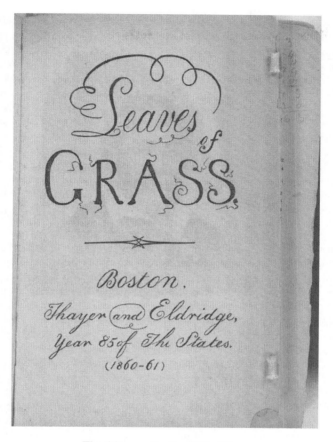

The title page for the 1860 edition

In spite of Whitman's commitment to revising and improving upon *Leaves of Green*, he also found time to continue writing against slavery. As the election of 1856 approached, he composed *The Eighteenth Presidency*, a pamphlet he failed to get published but contained a treatise "To the American Young Men, Mechanics, Farmers, Boatmen, Manufacturers, &C., of Virginia, Delaware, Maryland, The Carolinas, Kentucky, Tennessee, Georgia, Alabama, Florida, Mississippi, Arkansas, Missouri, Louisiana and Texas." In it, he goaded readers by asking them, "How much longer do you intend to submit to the espionage and terrorism of the three hundred and fifty thousand owners of slaves? Are you too their slaves, and their most obedient slaves? Shall no one among you dare open his mouth to say he is opposed to slavery, as a man should be, on account of the whites, and wants it abolished for their sake? Is not a writer, speaker, teacher to be left alive, but those who lick up the spit that drops from the mouths of the three hundred and fifty thousand masters? Is there hardly one free, courageous soul left in fifteen large and populous States? Do the ranks of the owners of slaves themselves contain no men desperate and tired of that service and sweat of the mind, worse than any service in sugar-fields or corn-fields, under the eyes of overseers? Do the three hundred and fifty thousand expect to bar off forever all preachers, poets, philosophers -- all that makes the brain of These States, free literature, free thought, the good old cause of liberty? Are they blind? Do they not see those unrelaxed circles of death narrowing and narrowing every hour around them?...You young men of the Southern States! is the word Abolitionist so hateful to you, then? Do you not know that Washington, Jefferson, Madison, and all the great Presidents and primal warriors and sages were declared abolitionists? You young men! American mechanics, farmers, boatmen, manufacturers, and all work-people of the South, the same as the North! you are either to abolish slavery, or it will abolish you."

While people who read those words today may assume that Whitman was a man of vision and equality when it came to issues of race, that was not the case. Authors George and David Hutchinson explained, "Whitman has commonly been perceived as one of the few white American writers who transcended the racial attitudes of his time, a great prophet celebrating ethnic and racial diversity and embodying egalitarian ideals. ... Nonetheless, the truth is that Whitman in person largely, though confusedly and idiosyncratically, internalized typical white racial attitudes of his time, place, and class...Whitman's racial attitudes were unstable and inconsistent. The inconsistencies particularly appear in differences between his journalism and unpublished notes, on the one hand, and his poetry and visionary essays on the other—as if Whitman did not trust himself on racial issues and therefore largely avoided them, or veiled his attitudes in the work by which he wanted to revitalize American culture and finally to be remembered as democracy's bard. Concerning people of African descent, what little is known about the early development of Whitman's racial awareness suggests he imbibed the prevailing white prejudices of his place and time, thinking of black people as servile, shiftless, ignorant, and given to stealing, although he would remember individual blacks of his youth in positive terms. His later experiences in the South apparently did nothing to mitigate early impressions, although readers of the twentieth century, including black ones, imagined him as a fervent antiracist."

With his internal conflicts matching those of the nation, Whitman greeted the start of the American Civil War enthusiastically with the publication of "Beat! Beat! Drums!"

> "Beat! beat! drums!—blow! bugles! blow!
> Through the windows—through doors—burst like a ruthless force,
> Into the solemn church, and scatter the congregation,
> Into the school where the scholar is studying;
> Leave not the bridegroom quiet—no happiness must he have now with

his bride,
Nor the peaceful farmer any peace, ploughing his field or gathering
    his grain,
So fierce you whirr and pound you drums—so shrill you bugles blow.

    Beat! beat! drums!—blow! bugles! blow!
Over the traffic of cities—over the rumble of wheels in the streets;
Are beds prepared for sleepers at night in the houses? no sleepers
    must sleep in those beds,
No bargainers' bargains by day—no brokers or speculators—would
    they continue?
Would the talkers be talking? would the singer attempt to sing?
Would the lawyer rise in the court to state his case before the judge?
Then rattle quicker, heavier drums—you bugles wilder blow.

    Beat! beat! drums!—blow! bugles! blow!
Make no parley—stop for no expostulation,
Mind not the timid—mind not the weeper or prayer,
Mind not the old man beseeching the young man,
Let not the child's voice be heard, nor the mother's entreaties,
Make even the trestles to shake the dead where they lie awaiting the
    hearses,
So strong you thump O terrible drums—so loud you bugles blow."

At 41, Whitman was safe from being drafted into military service, but his younger brother, George, enlisted and soon began sending home detailed descriptions of both battles and life in camp. Then, in December 1862, the name "G. W. Whitmore" was listed among the wounded soldiers published in the *New York Tribune*. Fearing that the name was actually a misprint and that his brother had fallen, Whitmore traveled to the area where he had last heard George's unit was stationed and began to check hospitals and camps. Thankfully, he found George alive and well, having suffered only a flesh wound.

In his 40s, Whitman was obviously a confirmed bachelor, he appears to have had at least some romantic relationships with women during this period. In 1862, he met Ellen Grey, an actress then performing in New York City. The two appear to have had a long term relationship that may or may not have included a child or two. Years later, Whitman claimed, "My life, young manhood, mid-age, times South, etc., have been jolly bodily, and doubtless open to criticism. Tho' unmarried I have had six children — two are dead — one living, Southern grandchild, fine boy, writes to me occasionally — circumstances (connected with their fortune and benefit) have separated me from intimate relations.'"

In many ways, the psychological impact that the war had on Whitman was greater than

George's physical wound. Over the course of the war, Whitman witnessed firsthand the horrors that plagued Civil War era hospitals, and he was so moved that he left New York and headed to Washington D. C., where he could serve in some sort of capacity to help the war effort. For most of 1863, Whitman divided his time between working at the Army paymaster's office and volunteering as a nurse in the local military hospitals.

In 1863, he wrote "The Great Army of the Sick," an article published in the *New York Times*. In it, he vividly described what he was seeing: "The military hospitals, convalescent camps, &c. in Washington and its neighborhood sometimes contain over fifty thousand sick and wounded men. Every form of wound, (the mere sight of some of them having been known to make a tolerably hardy visitor faint away,) every kind of malady, like a long procession, with typhoid fever and diarrhoea at the head as leaders, are here in steady motion. The soldier's hospital! how many sleepless nights how many woman's tears, how many long and aching hours and days of suspense, from every one of the Middle, Eastern and Western States, have concentrated here!...Upon a few of these hospitals I have been almost daily calling as a missionary, on my own account, for the sustenance and consolation of some of the most needy cases of sick and dying men, for the last two months. One has much to learn in order to do good in these places. Great tact is required. These are not like other hospitals. By far the greatest proportion (I should say five-sixths) of the patients are American young men, intelligent, of independent spirit, tender feelings, used to a hardy and healthy life; largely the farmers are represented by their sons -- largely the mechanics and workingmen of the cities. Then they are soldiers. All these points must be borne in mind."

Whitman's graphic depictions shocked the public in much the same way that *Leaves of Grass* had, albeit for different reasons. He soon found himself battling with his superiors and had to appeal to Emerson to find a new job. He continued to struggle throughout the rest of 1864, during which George was taken prisoner and his brother Andrew died after a long struggle with alcoholism and tuberculosis. Whitman was also compelled to commit a third brother, Jesse, to a mental hospital.

Fortunately, things were looking up in January 1865. With the help of his friend and fellow poet, William Douglas O'Connor, Whitman finally found work at the Bureau of Indian Affairs. A month later, George was released by the Confederates and allowed to return home.

The war ended in April and May 1865, and Whitman published *Drum-Taps*, a collection of 53 poems he wrote before and during the war, on May 1. The title poem began with an almost apologetic recollection of his first patriotic feelings:

"FIRST, O songs, for a prelude,

Lightly strike on the stretch'd tympanum, pride and joy in my city,

How she led the rest to arms—how she gave the cue,

How at once with lithe limbs, unwaiting a moment, she sprang;

(O superb! O Manhattan, my own, my peerless!

O strongest you in the hour of danger, in crisis! O truer than steel!)

How you sprang! how you threw off the costumes of peace with indifferent hand;

How your soft opera-music changed, and the drum and fife were heard in their stead;

How you led to the war, (that shall serve for our prelude, songs of soldiers,)

How Manhattan drum-taps led."

Then, in the middle, he observed, "All the mutter of preparation—all the determin'd arming; The hospital service—the lint, bandages, and medicines; The women volunteering for nurses—the work begun for, in earnest—no mere parade now; War! an arm'd race is advancing!—the welcome for battle—no turning away; War! be it weeks, months, or years—an arm'd race is advancing to welcome it."

Ultimately, though, the war was won, so he ended on a high note:

"And you, Lady of Ships! you Mannahatta!

Old matron of this proud, friendly, turbulent city!

Often in peace and wealth you were pensive, or covertly frown'd amid all your children;

But now you smile with joy, exulting old Mannahatta!

The rest of the poems were largely martial in nature, consisting of such titles are "Cavalry crossing the ford," and "By the bivouac's fitful flame."

Drum-Taps proved very popular, and less than two months later, Whitman released *Sequel to Drum Taps*, a collection of 18 additional poems concerning the Civil War. Among these was his most famous work, and one of the most famous poems in American history, "O Captain! My Captain!" The poem is a moving tribute to the recently assassinated President Lincoln:

"O Captain! My Captain! our fearful trip is done;
The ship has weather'd every rack, the prize we sought is won;

The port is near, the bells I hear, the people all exulting,
While follow eyes the steady keel, the vessel grim and daring:

But O heart! heart! heart!

O the bleeding drops of red,

Where on the deck my Captain lies,

Fallen cold and dead.

O Captain! My Captain! rise up and hear the bells;
Rise up—for you the flag is flung—for you the bugle trills;
For you bouquets and ribbon'd wreaths—for you the shores a-crowding;
For you they call, the swaying mass, their eager faces turning;

Here captain! dear father!

This arm beneath your head;

It is some dream that on the deck,

You've fallen cold and dead.

My Captain does not answer, his lips are pale and still;
My father does not feel my arm, he has no pulse nor will;
The ship is anchor'd safe and sound, its voyage closed and done;
From fearful trip, the victor ship, comes in with object won;

Exult, O shores, and ring, O bells!

But I, with mournful tread,

Walk the deck my captain lies,

Fallen cold and dead."

According to historian William A. Pannapacker, "Whitman was deeply moved by Lincoln's death on Good Friday, 14 April 1865. It was a personal tragedy, but it also seemed like the culminating sacrifice of an epic poem. Drum-Taps was incomplete without some concluding tribute to Lincoln. ... 'O Captain!' describes the poet's grief for the Union's fallen helmsman in uncharacteristically conventional verse."

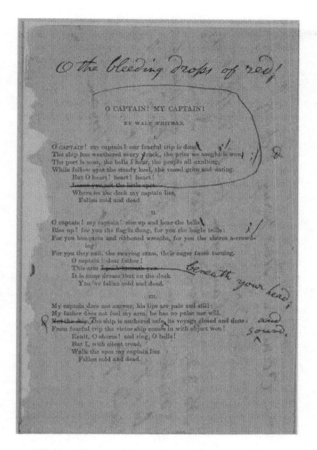

Whitman's noted for a revised version of the poem

A handwritten draft of the poem

Ironically, "O Captain!" may have ultimately saved Whitman's career, as Pannapacker noted: "The Lincoln poems, particularly "O Captain!," were received indulgently; they helped to make the controversial author of Leaves more acceptable to genteel readers. With the aid of supporters like William D. O'Connor, Whitman promoted himself as an authority on Lincoln, a comparable type, and even the object of Lincoln's admiration. Whitman's lecture on the assassination at Ford's Theater, "Death of Abraham Lincoln," was an annual rite between 1879 and 1890 in which Lincoln became America's mythical "Martyr Chief," and Whitman became the Good Gray Poet (Prose Works 2:509). Whitman thought "O Captain!" to be one of his weaker poems and often tired of reading it. … Like Washington, Lincoln had entered the American civil religion, and Whitman submitted to demands for a conventional elegist. It was a profitable venture, for it kept Whitman before the public long enough to reveal the value of his other works."

For better or worse, Whitman soon had more time to devote to his writing. On June 30, 1865, the new Secretary of the Interior, Senator James Harlan, let Whitman go from his position with the Bureau of Indian Affairs. While Harlan fired a number of men at the time, many believe that his dismissal had something to do with *Leaves of Grass.*

Harlan

O'Connor stepped in and persuaded those in charge to find Whitman another government position, this time with the Office of the Attorney General. O'Connor also wrote a very flattering biographical sketch of his friend entitled *The Good Gray Poet: A Vindication.* In it, he exclaimed, "On the 30th of June last, this true American man and author was dismissed, under circumstances of peculiar wrong, from a clerkship he had held for six months in the Department of the Interior. … Upon the interrogation of an eminent officer of the Government…Mr. Harlan averred that Walt Whitman had been in no way remiss in the discharge of his duties, but that, on the contrary, so far as he could learn, his conduct had been most exemplary. Indeed, during the few months of his tenure of office, he had been promoted. The sole and only cause of his dismissal, Mr. Harlan said, was that he had written the book of poetry entitled *Leaves of Grass*. This book Mr. Harlan characterized as 'full of indecent passages.' The author, he said, was 'a very bad man,' a 'free lover.' Argument being had upon these propositions, Mr. Harlan was, as regards the book, utterly unable to maintain his assertions, and, as regards the author, was forced to own that his opinion of him had been changed. Nevertheless, after this substantial admission of his injustice, he absolutely refused to revoke his action."

Among Whitman's favorite duties at the Attorney General's office was reviewing applications from Confederate soldiers for pardons that would clear them from federal charges related to their wartime activities. He wrote to a friend, "I am in that part of the office where pardons are attended to. There is a stream of rebels passing in all the time to be pardoned. ... There are some real characters among them, and you know I have a fancy for anything out of the ordinary. A good many women come up to Washington to look after pardons. All are dressed in deep black. Then there are bushels of applications arriving by every mail."

Later Years

Whitman in later years

"The United States themselves are essentially the greatest poem." – Walt Whitman

During the post-war years, Whitman formed one of the closest relationships of his life. In 1866, he met a bus conductor named Peter Doyle. In speaking of their first meeting, Doyle used language and terms more in keeping with a burgeoning love story than a platonic friendship: "The night was very stormy...the storm was awful. Walt had his blanket — it was thrown round his shoulders — he seemed like an old sea-captain. He was the only passenger, it was a lonely night, so I thought I would go in and talk with him. Something in me made me do it and something in him drew me that way. He used to say there was something in me had the same effect on him. Anyway, I went into the car. We were familiar at once — I put my hand on his knee — we understood. He did not get out at the end of the trip — in fact went all the way back with me. I think the year of this was 1866. From that time on we were the biggest sort of friends. . . . Walt rode with me often — often at noon, always at night. He rode round with me on the last trip — sometimes rode for several trips. Everybody knew him. He had a way of taking the measure of the drivers' hands — had calf-skin gloves made for them every winter in Georgetown — these gloves were his personal presents to the men. He saluted the men on the other cars as we passed — threw up his hand. They cried to him, ' Hullo, Walt ! ' and he would reply, ' Ah, there ! ' or something like. He was welcome always as the flowers in May. Everybody appreciated his attentions, and he seemed to appreciate our attentions to him."

The two men lived together for the rest of Whitman's stay in Washington, in spite of the fact that Doyle was 30 years Whitman's junior. They were even photographed together, an unusual move in that era. That said, there is no evidence from Whitman's own hand indicating they were lovers. Considering the manner in which he flouted all social conventions of the time, this seems odd, but it is important to remember that real evidence of any homosexual activity could have very well landed them in jail, and he may have been too smart to let that happen.

Whitman and Doyle

By the summer of 1866, Whitman's job and reputation were secure enough to allow him to take a leave of absence for a month. He used the time to revise *Leaves of Grass* yet again, this time including poetry from the war years, but he still had difficulty finding someone willing to publish the controversial work. As a result, the next edition was not released until 1867. With this work completed, Whitman thought he was finally done with *Leaves*. However, the book would prove to be his closest companion for the rest of his life.

Having grown tired of ongoing struggles to find American publishers for his poetry, Whitman appealed to those across the Atlantic, and in February 1868, a British publisher released *Poems of Walt Whitman*. William Rossetti, the book's English editor, carefully selected the poems to be included, which disappointed Whitman. He wrote to a friend, "My feeling and attitude about a volume of selections from my Leaves by Mr. Rosetti, for London publication, are simply passive ones—yet with decided satisfaction that if the job is to be done, it is to be by such hands. Perhaps, too, "good-natured," as you advise—certainly not ill-natured. I wish Mr. Rosetti to know that I appreciate his appreciation, realize his delicacy & honor, & warmly thank him for his literary friendliness. I have no objection to his substituting other words—leaving it all to his own tact, &c.—for "onanist," "father-stuff" &c. Briefly, I hereby empower him, (since that seems to be the pivotal affair, & since he has the kindness to shape his action so much by my wishes—& since, indeed, the sovereignty of the responsibility is not at all mine in the case,)—to make verbal changes of that sort, wherever, for reasons sufficient to him, he decides that they are indispensable. I would add that it is a question with me whether the introductory essay or prose preface to the first edition is worth printing."

Ultimately, the book was crucially acclaimed, especially after the popular author Anne Gilchrist recommended it to those in her literary circles. In fact, the book was so popular that it inspired Whitman to issue yet another revised edition of *Leaves of Grass*. Published in 1871, an unfounded rumor of his death helped sales and made the book popular around the world.

In their biography of Whitman, Schyberg and Allen explained, "Whitman is the American poet. It is not going too far to say that through him America first achieved a position in world literature. … Walt Whitman broke with European academic tradition in both style and content, and he was fully aware of it. That was part of his program. He celebrated modern reality, modern America and her democracy. …he introduced 'the divine average' into literature. Whitman's complaint against both earlier and contemporary literature is that it was written for a minority, an elite few. No writer, he said…had spoken straight to the people or had created a single work especially for them. In 'Song of the Exposition,' 1871, he declared his poetic intention 'to teach the average man the glory of his daily walk and trade.'"

Satisfied that he finally had enough money to live on, Whitman left his job at the Attorney General's office in January 1872 and spent the rest of the year caring for his ailing mother. He also received special recognition when Dartmouth College invited him to give the commencement address that June.

In 1873, Whitman suffered a severe stroke that left him semi-paralyzed for the rest of his life. Unable to continue to care for himself, he was forced to move in with his younger brother, George, who had become an engineer after the war. He would live at the younger brother's home on 431 Stevens Street in Camden, New Jersey, for more than a decade.

Whitman's home in Camden

Compounding his grief over his own health was the loss of his mother in May 1873. He fell into a deep depression, and rumors spread that he was being consumed by his sorrow. This is perhaps the reason why, in 1874, some members of the local Spiritualism movement, thinking that Whitman must surely be a kindred spirit, invited him to write a poem on their behalf. They were less than pleased when he responded, "Your notes inviting me to write about Spiritualism reached me during a late severe spell of illness, which will account for their not being answered at the time. I thank you for your courtesy, but I am neither disposed nor able to write anything about this so-called Spiritualism. (It seems to me nearly altogether a poor, cheap, crude humbug.)"

As is so often the case, Whitman's personal sorrow opened up the floodgates for his writing, and the years he lived with his brother were some of the most productive of his life. He revised *Leaves of Grass* twice, once in 1876 and again in 1881.

The frontispiece for the edition of *Leaves of Grass* that was published in 1883

As far as Whitman's personal life was concerned, he formed a new (and possibly romantic) relationship during this period. While living in Camden, Whitman met a teenager named Bill Duckett who lived up the street. Duckett apparently performed various odd jobs for Whitman, and when he moved to his own home at 328 Mickle Street, Duckett and his grandmother, Lydia Watson, followed, renting a small apartment a few doors down. While it is true that the men spent a good bit of time together, Whitman's own words in no way hint of a sexual relationship. For instance, in an 1885 interview, he told someone, "I go out every day in my carriage, and a friend of mine, Willie Duckett, a neighbor's little boy, always comes and goes with me."

Whitman and Duckett

One man who was more likely a lover of Whitman's was Harry Stafford. Whitman met Stafford in 1876, when Stafford was 18. According to Whitman expert Arnie Kantrowitz, "Walt Whitman...still recovering from his stroke of 1873, came to the office to work on the Centennial edition of Leaves of Grass, and the two began one of the most intense relationships of the poet's life. Stafford took Whitman to visit his parents at White Horse Farm, near Kirkwood, New Jersey. ... [Whitman] also found time to meet there with a Stafford farm hand named Ed Cattell, but he kept those encounters secret from Stafford. Stafford and Whitman slept together in the same top floor bedroom, and when they traveled together Whitman referred to him as 'my nephew' and insisted that they be accommodated in the same bed. Whitman's friend John Burroughs complained that they 'cut up like two boys,' and he found their frolicsome behavior annoying. The Stafford family, however, were pleased to see the well-known man act as mentor to their son and gladly forgave any bad manners, chalking them up to artistic temperament. They hung a picture of the poet on their sitting room wall."

Kantrowitz continued, "Despite the frolicking, the relationship was a stormy one. They quarreled frequently, and several times Stafford returned a friendship ring given to him by Whitman. Stafford wrote that there was 'something wanting to compleete [sic] our friendship,' perhaps meaning sexual relations. At another time, he wrote of wanting to buy a suit of clothes like Whitman's so he could earn the admiration of his friends. He also wrote, 'I am thinking of what I am shielding, I want to try and make a man of myself' (qtd. in Miller 6), perhaps referring to guilt about homosexuality or simply to immaturity."

Ultimately, Kantrowitz concluded, "Stafford went from one job to another until he returned to the family farm. He and Whitman remained close until Stafford married Eva Westcott in 1884, after which the poet visited occasionally. When he died, Whitman left Stafford his silver watch, originally intended for Peter Doyle."

Not long after Stafford married, Whitman entered into his final long term relationship, bringing a middle aged widow, Mary Oakes Davis, into his home to care for him. While she may only have served as his housekeeper, their relationship was certainly a warm one, for she served him without pay for the rest of his life, while he offered her a home for not only herself but also a menagerie of pets that she cherished. Still, as Whitman scholar Carol Singley noted, "Critics agree that Whitman—crippled and increasingly dependent—greatly benefited from Davis's services. … The fairness of Whitman's bargain with the housekeeper is less clear. The arrangement apparently favored Whitman: Davis received no wages for her work and…claimed after Whitman's death that she had paid most of the grocery bills. … The precise nature of Whitman and Davis's relationship is also a matter of speculation. … Davis's strongest defender is Whitman's nurse, Elizabeth Leavitt Keller, who portrays Davis as selflessly devoted to Whitman and subject to his manipulations as well as to neighbors' gossip about an unmarried couple living together. Whitman's arrangement with Davis required mutual accommodation: she rendered loyal service but little understood the poet's idiosyncrasies or genius; he acknowledged her care but may have underestimated its value."

Whitman may have not paid Davis because he did not have the money to do so, for there were rumors that he was broke. In 1885, concerned for his welfare, Gilchrist wrote to Whitman:

"My Dearest Friend:

"A kind of anxiety has for some time past weighed upon me and upon others, I find, who love & admire you, that you do not have all the comforts you ought to have; that you are perhaps sometimes straightened for means. We have had letters from several young men, almost or quite strangers to us, asking questions on this subject; and we hoped & thought that if this were so, you would permit those who have received such priceless gifts from you to put their gratitude into some tangible shape, some 'free-will offering.' Hence the paragraph was put into the Athenaeum which I send with this, and we were proceeding to organize our forces when your paper came to hand this morning (the Camden Post, July 3), which seems decisively to bid us desist. Or at all events wait till we had told you of our wishes and plan. One thing would, I feel sure, give you pleasure in any case; and that is to know that there is over here a little band—perhaps indeed it is now quite a considerable one, for we had not yet had time to ascertain how considerable—who would joyfully respond to that Poem of yours, 'To Rich Givers.'"

A portrait of Whitman in the late 1880s

In 1891, Whitman released his final edition of *Leaves of Grass*, one that is now known as the "Deathbed Edition." Of it, he wrote to a friend, "L. of G. at last complete—after 33 y'rs of hackling at it, all times & moods of my life, fair weather & foul, all parts of the land, and peace & war, young & old."

In keeping with his belief that death was coming, Whitman used much of the money he earned from this edition to have a granite mausoleum built for himself. He carefully oversaw its construction, and he was laid to rest there following his death on March 26, 1892. Doctors who performed the autopsy were shocked by what they discovered - Whitman's lungs at the time of his death were functioning at only one-eighth capacity, due in part to a final bout with pneumonia, and the doctors discovered a large tumor had eaten through one of his ribs, which must have been causing excruciating pain. Indeed, near the end, Whitman had written, "I suffer all the time: I have no relief, no escape: it is monotony—monotony—monotony—in pain."

For all his scandalous behavior and personal idiosyncrasies, Whitman died a celebrity, and his Camden home could barely hold the 1,000 visitors that passed by his oak coffin to pay their respects with quiet words and wreaths of flowers. Four days after his death, Whitman was buried in his tomb at Harleigh Cemetary. At a public ceremony at the cemetery, friends of his delivered speeches while the gathered mourners were treated to live music and refreshments. Robert Ingersoll, the noted orator and agnostic, eulogized his deceased friend. Sometime afterwards, Whitman was joined in his eternal repose by the remains of his parents, two of his brothers and their families.

Ingersoll

Walt Whitman is often spoken of as America's national poet, being to the United States what Tennyson was to England. Various writers and scholars have offered their evaluation in trying to define what makes Whitman so American. D.H. Lawrence once wrote, "Whitman is one of the greatest of the Americans, one of the greatest poets of the world. He has gone farther, in actual living expression, than any man, it seems to me. Dostoevsky has burrowed underground into the decomposing psyche. But Whitman has gone forward in life-knowledge. It is he who surmounts the grand climacteric of our civilization. He really arrives at that stage of infinity which seers sought. By subjecting the deepest centers of the lower self he attains the maximum consciousness in the higher self: a degree of ex tensive consciousness greater than any man in the modern world."

Danish biographers Frederik Schyberg and Evie Allison Allen asserted, "Unless we clearly realize Whitman's absolutely religious belief in Leaves of Grass we cannot understand him. With this understanding, much about him that seemed ludicrous and trivial before becomes explicable and forgivable. He invented myths about himself to conceal the periods of his life in which nothing particular had happened to him (and not much did happen to Whitman; it was in his inner life that the greatest and finest things always took place and were transformed into poetry) or in which he had been overcome by innate weakness of character. Was it not a very human concealment of what he thought concerned him and him only? What concern was it of his readers? Especially when he had fought his way through and was done with his past life? Thus, his naïvely vain preoccupation with his own mausoleum during his last years--which suggests immediately an amusing comparison with his contemporary Mary Baker Eddy, the talented founder of Christian Science--becomes only a consistent and sustained effort to establish the official portrait of Walt Whitman the eminent American poet. And then there is the astounding and ingenuous self-advertising in anonymous reviews and character sketches written by himself, which Symonds and Perry had already noted and which Holloway has made one of his chief tasks to discover--and has found a surprisingly large number of examples in the contemporary American newspapers. Subterfuges of this sort, so regrettable to Europeans, throw a somewhat humorous light on the insatiable vanity which made them possible, but they also reveal the sublime faith in himself that enabled Whitman to produce the great book Leaves of Grass. This method, for better or for worse, is fundamentally as American as is the book itself."

One Whitman scholar, Stephen John Mack, tells critics to look to Whitman's nationalism. "Whitman's seemingly mawkish celebrations of the United States [are] one of those problematic features of his works that teachers and critics read past or explain away."

In his essay "Walt Whitman's Nationalism in the First Edition of Leaves of Grass", Nathanael O'Reilly summarized Whitman's view of his country: "Whitman's imagined America is arrogant, expansionist, hierarchical, racist and exclusive; such an America is unacceptable to Native Americans, African-Americans, immigrants, the disabled, the infertile, and all those who value equal rights."

Whitman's view of America reflected the views of most of his countrymen at the time that the country was a place for whites of Anglo-Saxon descent and (broadly) Protestant sensibilities. While his poems expressed egalitarian ideals, it was equality for one group only and did not necessarily intend to include anyone outside that group, a phenomenon historians have noted in the political rhetoric of the 19th century. In his poetry, Whitman reflected rather than challenged America's racial attitudes. As George Hutchinson and David Drews wrote in their essay on Whitman's racial attitudes, "Because of the radically democratic and egalitarian aspects of his poetry, readers generally expect, and desire for, Whitman to be among the literary heroes that transcended the racist pressures that abounded in all spheres of public discourse during the nineteenth century. He did not, at least not consistently; nonetheless his poetry has been a model for democratic poets of all nations and races, right up to our own day. How Whitman could have been so prejudiced, and yet so effective in conveying an egalitarian and antiracist sensibility in his poetry, is a puzzle yet to be adequately addressed."

Nonetheless, despite his shortcomings, Walt Whitman has often been labeled as America's first "poet of democracy," a title meant to reflect his ability to write in a singularly American character. A British friend of his, Mary Smith Whitall Costelloe, wrote, "You cannot really understand America without Walt Whitman, without Leaves of Grass... He has expressed that civilization, 'up to date,' as he would say, and no student of the philosophy of history can do without him."

Literary critic Harold Bloom summed it all up well in the introduction for the 150th anniversary of Leaves of Grass: "If you are American, then Walt Whitman is your imaginative father and mother, even if, like myself, you have never composed a line of verse. You can nominate a fair number of literary works as candidates for the secular Scripture of the United States. They might include Melville's Moby-Dick, Twain's Adventures of Huckleberry Finn, and Emerson's two series of Essays and The Conduct of Life. None of those, not even Emerson's, are as central as the first edition of Leaves of Grass."

Online Resources

Other books about poets by Charles River Editors

Other books about Walt Whitman on Amazon

Bibliography

Callow, Philip. *From Noon to Starry Night: A Life of Walt Whitman*. Chicago: Ivan R. Dee, 1992.

Kaplan, Justin. *Walt Whitman: A Life*. New York: Simon and Schuster, 1979.

Loving, Jerome. *Walt Whitman: The Song of Himself*. University of California Press, 1999.

Miller, James E., Jr. *Walt Whitman*. New York: Twayne Publishers, Inc. 1962

Reynolds, David S. *Walt Whitman's America: A Cultural Biography*. New York: Vintage Books, 1995.

Stacy, Jason. *Walt Whitman's Multitudes: Labor Reform and Persona in Whitman's Journalism and the First 'Leaves of Grass', 1840–1855*. New York: Peter Lang Publishing, 2008.

Free Books by Charles River Editors

We have brand new titles available for free most days of the week. To see which of our titles are currently free, click on this link.

Discounted Books by Charles River Editors

We have titles at a discount price of just 99 cents everyday. To see which of our titles are currently 99 cents, click on this link.

Made in the USA
Middletown, DE
19 February 2025

71468936R00026